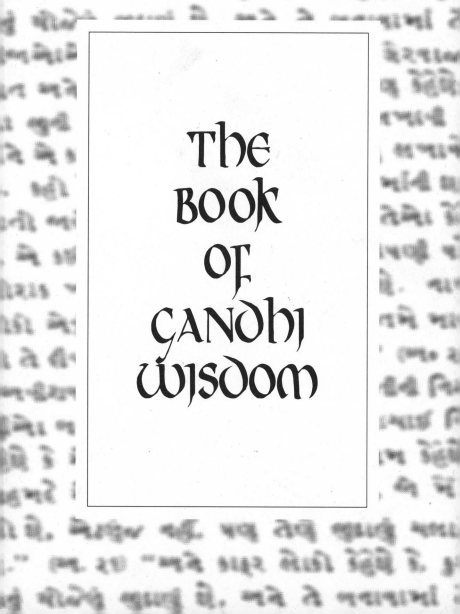

The
Book
Of
Gandhi
Wisdom

THE BOOK OF GANDHI WISDOM

Compiled by
Trudy S. Settel

A Citadel Press Book
Published by Carol Publishing Group

Material for this book was gathered from print and broadcast media around the world that have reported Gandhi's speeches and writings. Permission to use the quotations in this book was granted by the Consulate General of India and by the Navajivan Trust of India.

A Citadel Press Book

Published by Carol Publishing Group

Citadel Press is a registered trademark of Carol Communications, Inc.

Editorial Offices: 600 Madison Avenue, New York, N.Y. 10022

Sales and Distribution Offices: 120 Enterprise Avenue, Secaucus, N.J. 07094

In Canada: Canadian Manda Group, One Atlantic Avenue, Suite 105, Toronto,
    Ontario M6K 3E7

Queries regarding rights and permissions should be addressed to
Carol Publishing Group, 600 Madison Avenue, New York, N.Y. 10022

Carol Publishing Group books are available at special discounts for bulk purchases, sales promotion, fund-raising, or educational purposes. Special editions can be created to specifications. For details, contact: Special Sales Department, Carol Publishing Group, 120 Enterprise Avenue, Secaucus, N.J. 07094

Designed by Andrew B. Gardner

Manufactured in the United States of America

10 9 8 7 6 5 4 3 2 1

Library of Congress Cataloging-in-Publication Data

Settel, Trudy S.
    The book of Gandhi wisdom / compiled by Trudy S. Settel.
        p.   cm.
    ISBN 0-8065-1622-4 (paperback)
1. Gandhi, Mahatma, 1869-1948—Quotations. 2. Gandhi, Mahatma, 1869-1948—
Philosophy I. Title
DS481.G3S4595 1995
954.03¢5¢092—dc20
                                                        94-45212
                                                            CIP

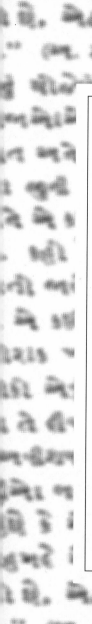

CONTENTS

5

INTRODUCTION

Mohandas Karamchand Gandhi was born in western India in 1869. He was not given the title "Mahatma," meaning "great soul," until later in life, in honor of his many achievements in the Indian movement for independence.

At nineteen Gandhi traveled to England to study law, then in 1893 accepted a job with the firm of Dada Abdulla and Company, a group of wealthy Mohammedan merchants in South Africa. The racially hostile climate of this country transformed him into a champion of civil rights for the Indian community. He introduced a policy of noncooperation with the civil authorities. *Satyagraha,* his principle of nonviolent action, combines the two Indian words *sat*, meaning truth, and *agraha*, meaning firmness, to signify that a man must declare the

7

truth and be willing to die for it without violence to anyone. This policy of nonviolence formed the basis of Gandhi's philosophy. While he also absorbed teachings from other religions, it was the Hindu scripture, the Bhagavad Gita, that became his bible. He would be considered the equivalent of a saint by his followers.

Gandhi's struggle for Indian civil rights was successful, prompting South African officials to reform their anti-Indian legislation. Impressed by Gandhi's ability to effect great social change without employing violence, the Indian Parliament invited him to return to India and present plans for their own self-government. In his home country, Gandhi's *satyagraha* campaign aroused interest, and many considered him a future political leader. He became an active member of the National Indian Congress. In turn, the leaders of the Congress expressed their confidence in Gandhi, asking him to revise their Constitution and legitimize the Congress as a countrywide political organization. Their plan succeeded with Gandhi's guidance, and the Congress remained the only political party in the country for years after independence. Under British rule, Gandhi carried on as a political agitator, dedicating himself to service to humanity and advocating conciliation among racial groups.

Gandhi's attempts to promote friendship between Hindus and Muslims incurred the wrath of Hindu fanatics, who considered the Muslims their enemies. When, due largely to Gandhi's pacifist efforts, independence finally became a reality, his political influence gradually declined. He was assassinated in 1948 by a Hindu fanatic who wanted to halt any reconciliation between Hindus and Muslims.

Gandhi's teachings profoundly influenced such reformers as Dr. Martin Luther King, Jr., Cesar Chavez, and Nelson Mandela, who, in June 1993, led a tribute to Mahatma Gandhi in the Natal province capital city (where Gandhi, after experiencing racial segregation on a train, developed the concept of *satyagraha*).

In shaping the policies of today's world leaders, Gandhi's philosophy has had a major impact on politicially troubled countries and will continue to affect the future of international politics. Compared by many to Christ for his teachings, his practice of nonviolence, and his tragic assassination, Gandhi remains a legendary figure of world history.

This anthology, drawn entirely from Gandhi's own words, brings to light the philosophical structure upon which the great man built his role in international affairs. Revealing his innermost thoughts and beliefs regarding man and the world, this inspirational material touches on the great concerns of humankind.

THE
SUTRAS

When
Truth is seen, there is
self-realization.

Worship Truth
at all times
with all your heart.

The highest Truth
cannot be perceived
in this life.

Nonviolence
is the highest Law.

Nonviolence is abstention
from causing pain to any creature
either in mind or body.
It also means love to all animals.
It is the protection of the cow,
For the cow symbolizes all animals.
It also comprises the brotherhood
of all men.

Love is indeed
the highest form
of nonviolence.
It is the basis of all domestic duties.

The world
is indeed the family of God.
Therefore the law of the family
should be the law
of the world.

Love
is the only remedy for hate.
It blossoms only in the heart
of a fearless man.

Satyagraha is the same as
truth force,
love force,
or soul force.

Nonviolence
is the eternal law; violence is only the
law of expediency.

15

By
his own suffering does a
brave man observe nonviolence.

The more one suffers,
the more one helps.
The purer the suffering,
the greater is the gain.

Falling
from his original state, man takes
birth, and falling still further,
he marries.
His salvation is only through
chastity.

Marriage
is for progeny and not
for sensual enjoyment.

Accumulation
of wealth
is accumulation of sin.

Always and
everywhere worship God in the poor.
Honor the ploughman,
And also the scavenger.

Art does not shine
by its external form alone.

The mere knowledge
of words and their meanings
is no education.

The body
is only the means
by which the soul manifests itself.

When cooperation
involves sin, noncooperation becomes
the highest duty.

If noncooperation is properly observed,
it grows into deep love.
If it is accompanied by violence,
it becomes sinful.
If it is devoid of violence,
it roots out sin.

Civil Disobedience would never lead
to anarchy or injustice.
For it is wedded to nonviolence.
There is no deceit nor disrespect
nor pride nor envy nor sin in it.

Truth,
purity, self-control, firmness,
fearlessness, humility, unity, peace,
and renunciation—these are the
inherent qualities of a civil resister.

A *satyagrahi*
has no enemies.
He discovers Truth by fasting
and prayer.
God alone is his abode, refuge,
and friend.

One perfect civil resister
is enough to root out injustice.

When we see
that we have gone wrong, it is our
duty to retrace our footsteps and
proceed again by the right path.

Violence on the part of the people
is to be feared more than
the violence of the rulers.

Prayer is not
an old woman's idle amusement.
Properly understood and applied,
it is the most potent instrument
of action.

Cowards
can never be moral.

Fear has its use,
but cowardice
has none.

The acquisition
of the spirit of nonresistance is a
matter of long training in self-denial
and appreciation of the hidden forces
within ourselves. It changes one's
outlook on life....It is the greatest
force because it is the highest
expression of the soul.

Truth
never damages a cause
that is just.

24

Coodness
must be joined with knowledge. Mere
goodness is not of much use, as I have
found in life. One must cultivate the
fine discriminating quality which goes
with spiritual courage and character.

A man
cannot serve God and Mammon,
nor be temperate and furious
at the same time.

A coward
is less than a man.
He does not deserve to be a member
of a society of men and women.

It is the law of love
that rules mankind.

Those who agree that
racial inequality must be removed
and yet do nothing to fight the evil
are impotent.

A reformer
has to sail not with the current. Very
often he has to go against it even
though it may cost him his life.

The mind
of a man who remains good under
compulsion cannot improve;
in fact, it worsens.

No one has the capacity
to judge God. We are drops in that
limitless ocean of mercy.

The music of life
is in danger of being lost
in the music of the voice.

God alone is the judge
of true greatness
because He knows men's hearts.

Just as one must not receive,
so must one not possess
anything which one
does not really need.

Love is the subtlest force
in the world.

One man cannot
do right in one department of life
whilst he is occupied in doing wrong
in any other department.
Life is one indivisible whole.

Absolute calm
is not the law of the ocean.
And it is the same
with the ocean of life.

I believe
that if one man gains spiritually,
the whole world gains with him,
and if one man falls
the whole world falls to that extent.

To a true artist,
only that face is beautiful which,
quite apart from its exterior,
shines with the truth within the soul.

Purity of life
is the highest and truest art.

Individual liberty
and interdependence
are both essential for life in society.

To call women the weaker sex is a libel; it is man's injustice to women.

I believe
that he is the true warrior who does not die killing but who has mastered the mantra of living by dying.

hatred can be overcome
only by love.
Counterhatred only increases the surface as well as the depth of hatred.

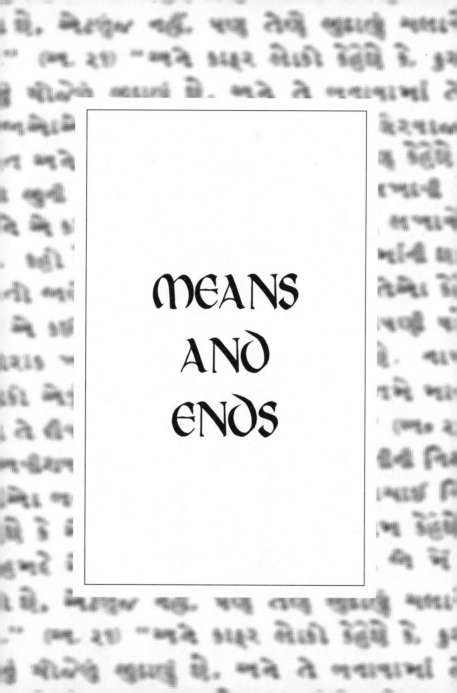

MEANS
AND
ENDS

They say "means are, after all, means." I would say "means are, after all, everything." As the means, so the end. There is no wall of separation between means and end.

I do not believe
in short-violent-cuts
to success.

The spiritual weapon of self-purification, intangible as it seems, is the most potent means of revolutionizing one's environment and loosening external shackles. It works subtly and invisibly; it is an intense process though it might often seem a weary and long-drawn process. It is the straightest way to liberation, the surest and quickest, and no effort can be too great for it. What it requires is faith—an unshakable mountainlike faith that flinches from nothing.

Your belief that there is no connection between the means and the end is a great mistake. Through that mistake, even men who have been considered religious have committed grievous crimes. Your reasoning is the same as saying that we can get a rose through planting a noxious weed. If I want to cross the ocean, I can do so only by means of a vessel; if I were to use a cart for that purpose, both the cart and I would soon find the bottom. "As is the God, so is the votary" is a maxim worth considering. Its meaning has been distorted, and men have gone astray. The means may be likened to a seed, the end to a tree; and there is just the same inviolable connection between the means and the end as there is between the seed and the tree. I am not likely to obtain the result flowing from the worship of God by laying myself prostrate before Satan. If, therefore, anyone were to say, "I want to worship God; it does not matter that I do so by means of Satan," it would be set down as ignorant folly.

We reap exactly as we sow.

The method of passive resistance is the clearest and safest, because, if the cause is not true, it is the resisters, and they alone, who suffer.

Freedom is not worth having if it does not connote freedom to err.

When Truth is seen, there is self-realization.

honest differences
are often a healthy sign of progress.

The weak can never forgive.
Forgiveness is
the attribute of the strong.

All crime is a kind of disease
and should be treated as such.

A no uttered from deepest conviction
is better and greater than a yes merely
uttered to please, or, what is worse,
to avoid trouble.

Anger and intolerance
are the twin enemies
of current understanding.

Impure thoughts
result in an impure end.

All forms of necessity
can contribute to man's freedom.
There is material and economic need.
There is spiritual need. The greatest of
man's spiritual needs is the need to be
delivered from the evil and falsity that
are in himself and in his society.

The real love
is to love them that hate you, to love
your neighbor even though you
distrust him.

Joy lives in the fight,
in the attempt,
in the suffering involved,
not in the victory itself.

It is beneath human dignity
to lose one's individuality and
become a mere cog in the machine.

Where there is love, there is life;
hatred leads to destruction.

Cood travels
at a snail's pace. Those who want to do
good are not selfish, they are not in a
hurry, they know that to impregnate
people with good requires a long time.

Religions are different roads
converging upon the same point.
What does it matter
that we take different roads,
so long as we reach the same goal?

Often does good come out of evil.
But that is not God's plan.
Man knows that
only evil can come out of evil,
as good out of good.

My writings
should be cremated with my body.
What I have done will endure,
not what I have said
and written.

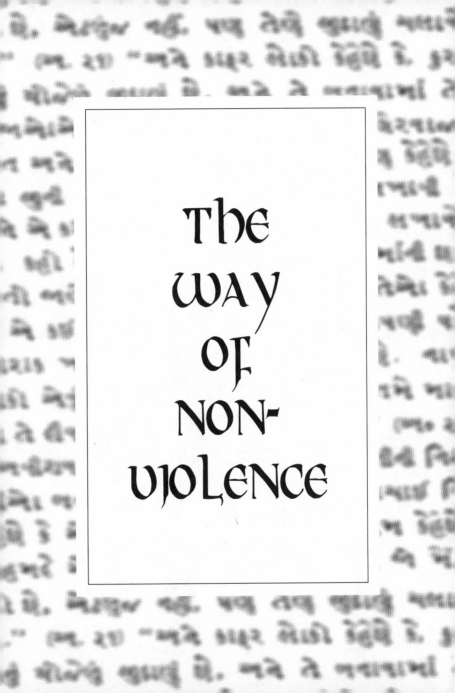

THE
WAY
OF
NON-
VIOLENCE

Nonviolence
is the greatest force at the disposal of
mankind. It is mightier than the
mightiest weapon of destruction
devised by the ingenuity of man.
Destruction is not the law of the
humans. Man lives freely by his
readiness to die, if need be, at the
hands of his brother, never by killing
him. Every murder or other injury, no
matter for what cause, committed or
inflicted on another is a crime
against humanity.

46

Perfect nonviolence
is impossible so long as we exist
physically, for we would want some
space at least to occupy.
Perfect nonviolence
whilst you are inhabiting the body
is only a theory,
like Euclid's point or straight line,
but we have to endeavor
every moment of our lives.

having flung aside the sword, there is nothing except the cup of love which I can offer to those who oppose me. It is by offering that cup that I expect to draw them close to me. I cannot think of permanent enmity between man and man, and believing as I do in the theory of rebirth, I live in the hope that, if not in this birth, in some other birth I shall be able to hug all humanity in friendly embrace.

Love is
the strongest force
the world possesses,
and yet it is the humblest imaginable.

The hardest heart
and the grossest ignorance
must disappear
before the rising sun of suffering
without anger
and without malice.

I am but a weak aspirant,
ever failing, ever trying. My failures
make me more vigilant than before
and intensify my faith.
I can see with the eye of faith that
the observance of the twin doctrines
of truth and nonviolence
has possibilities of which we have
but very inadequate conception.

I am
but a humble explorer
of the science of nonviolence.
Its hidden depths
sometimes stagger me
just as much as they stagger
fellow workers.

The first condition of nonviolence
is justice all round
in every department of life.
Perhaps it is too much
to expect of human nature.
I do not, however, think so.
No one should dogmatize about
the capacity of human nature
for degradation or exaltation.

It is no nonviolence
if we merely love those who love us.
It is nonviolence only when we love
those who hate us. I know how
difficult it is to follow this grand law
of love. But are not all great and good
things difficult to do? Love of the
hater is the most difficult of all. But
by the grace of God, even this most
difficult thing becomes easy to
accomplish if we want
to do it.

I saw that nations,
like individuals, could only be made
through the agony of the Cross
and in no other way.
Joy comes not
out of infliction of pain on others
but out of pain voluntarily borne
by oneself.

No man could be actively nonviolent
and not rise against social injustice,
no matter where it occurred.

54

Man and his deed are two distinct things. It is quite proper to resist and attack a system, but to resist and attack its author is tantamount to resisting and attacking oneself. For we are all tarred with the same brush and are children of one and the same Creator, and as such the divine powers within us are infinite. To slight a single human being is to slight those divine powers and thus to harm not only that being but with him the whole world.

Nonviolence
is a power which can be wielded
equally by all—children, young men
and women, or grown-up people—
provided they have a living faith in
the God of Love and have therefore
equal love for all mankind. When
nonviolence is accepted as the law of
life, it must pervade the whole being
and not be applied to isolated acts.

Jf we are to be nonviolent,
we must then not wish
for anything on this earth
which the meanest or the lowest
of human beings cannot have.

Nonviolence
implies voluntary submission
to the penalty for
noncooperation with evil.

A nonviolent man
can do nothing save by the power and
grace of God. Without it he will not
have the courage to die without anger,
without fear, and without retaliation.
Such courage
comes from the belief
that God sits in the hearts of all
and that there should be no fear
in the presence of God.

The moral to be legitimately drawn
from the supreme tragedy
of the bomb
is that it will not be
destroyed by counterbombs,
even as violence cannot be
by counterviolence.

Mankind
has to get out of violence
only through nonviolence.

Love is
a rare herb that makes a friend
even of a sworn enemy,
and this herb grows
out of nonviolence.

True nonviolence
is an impossibility
without the possession
of unadulterated fearlessness.

It is the acid test of nonviolence that in a nonviolent conflict there is no rancor left behind and, in the end, the enemies are converted into friends.

Truth (*satya*) implies love, and firmness (*agraha*) engenders and therefore serves as a synonym for force. I thus began to call the Indian movement *satyagraha;* that is to say, the force which is born of truth and love or nonviolence.

]do believe
that where there is only a choice
between cowardice and violence,
I would advise violence.
Hence also do I advocate training
in arms for those who believe
in the method of violence.
I would rather have India resort to
arms in order to defend her honor
than that she should
in a cowardly manner
become or remain a helpless witness
to her own dishonor.

Nonviolence
in its dynamic condition
means conscious suffering.
It does not mean meek submission
to the will of the evildoer,
but it means the pitting
of one's whole soul
against the will of the tyrant.

The force of nonviolence
is infinitely more wonderful and
subtle than the material forces of
nature, like electricity.

however much I may sympathize
with and admire worthy motives,
I am an uncompromising opponent of
violent methods even to serve
the noblest of causes.
Experience convinces me that
permanent good can never be
the outcome of untruth and violence.

Adaptability is not imitation.
It means the power of resistance
and assimilation.

64

Noncooperation is
a protest against
an unwitting
and unwilling
participation in evil.

If love or nonviolence
be not the law of our being,
the whole of my argument
falls to pieces.

In nonviolence
the masses have a weapon which
enables a child, a woman, or even a
decrepit old man to resist the
mightiest government successfully.
If your spirit is strong,
mere lack of physical strength
ceases to be a handicap.

It is a bad outlook
for the world if the spirit of violence
takes hold of the mass mind.
Ultimately it destroys the race.

Nonviolence is not a garment
to be put on and off
at will.
Its seat is in the heart,
and it must be an inseparable {part}
of our very being.

SELF-DISCIPLINE

To seek God,
one need not go on a pilgrimage
or light lamps fed with ghee
and burn incense
before the image of the deity
or anoint it or paint it with vermilion.
For He resides in our hearts.
If we could humbly obliterate in us
the consciousness of our physical body,
we would see Him
face to face.

I have learnt
through bitter experience
the one supreme lesson
to conserve my anger,
and as heat conserved
is transmuted into energy,
even so our anger controlled
can be transmuted into a power
which can move
the world.

Silence of the sewn-up lips
is no silence. One may achieve the
same result by chopping off one's
tongue, but that too would not be
silence. He is silent who,
having the capacity to speak,
utters no idle word.

Self-respect
and honor cannot be protected by
others. They are for each individual
himself or herself to guard.

Sex urge
is a fine and noble thing. There is
nothing to be ashamed of in it. But it
is meant only for the act of creation.
Any other use of it is a sin
against God and humanity.

My prayerful search
gave me the revealing maxim
"Truth is God"
instead of the usual one, "
God is Truth."

I know from my own experience
that as long as I looked
upon my wife carnally,
we had no real understanding.
Our love did not reach a high plane.
There was affection between us always,
but we came closer and closer
the more we, or rather I,
became restrained.
There never was any want
of restraint on the part of my wife.
Very often she would show restraint,

but she rarely resisted me
although she showed disinclination
very often.
All the time I wanted carnal pleasure
I could not serve her.
The moment I bade goodbye
to a life of carnal pleasure,
our whole relationship
became spiritual.
Lust died
and love reigned instead.

It is better to enjoy
through the body than to be
enjoying the thought of it. It is good
to disapprove of sensual desires
as soon as they arise in the mind and
try to keep them down; but
if, for want of physical enjoyment,
the mind wallows in thoughts
of enjoyment, then it is legitimate
to satisfy the hunger of the body.
About this I have no doubt.

Civilization,
in the real sense of the term, consists
not in the multiplication
but in the deliberate and voluntary
restriction of wants.
This alone promotes real happiness
and contentment and increases
the capacity for service.

Noncooperation with evil
is as much a duty as is
cooperation with good.

Prayer from the heart
can achieve
what nothing else can
in the world.

God alone knows
the mind of a person;
and the duty of a man of God
is to act as he is directed
by his inner voice.
I claim that I act accordingly.

I ask nobody to follow me.
Everyone should follow
his own inner voice.

No man, if he is pure, has anything
more precious to give than his life.

Hinduism rules out indulgences
and multiplication of wants,
as these hamper one's growth
to the ultimate identity
with the Universal Self.

Moral support
cannot really be given
in the sense of giving.
It automatically comes
to he who is qualified to take it.
And such a one can take it
in abundance.

Silence becomes cowardice
when occasion demands
speaking out the whole truth
and acting accordingly.

Intellectual work is important
and has an undisputed place
in the scheme of life.
But what I insist on is
the necessity of physical labor.
No man, I claim, ought to be free
from that obligation.

Rights that do not flow
from duty well performed
are not worth having.

I could not be leading a religious life unless I identified myself with the whole of mankind, and that I could not do unless I took part in politics. The whole gamut of man's activities today constitutes an indivisible whole. You cannot divide social, economic, political, and purely religious work into watertight compartments. Receive his blows as though they were so many flowers. Even one such man, if God favors him, can do the work of a thousand.

Let us be clear
regarding the language we use
and the thoughts we nurture.
For what is language
but the expression of thought?

My imperfections
and failures
are as much a blessing from God
as my successes and my talents,
and I lay them both
at His feet.

83

So long
as we have not cultivated
the strength to die
with courage and love in our hearts,
we cannot hope to develop
the ahimsa of the strong.

Man easily capitulates
when sin is presented
in the garb of virtue.

To forget how to dig the earth
and tend the soil
is to forget ourselves.

Chastity
is one of the greatest disciplines.

A nation that is capable of limitless
sacrifice is capable of rising to
limitless heights. The purer the
sacrifice, the quicker the progress.

In mass civil resistance, leadership is essential; in individual civil resistance, every resister is his own leader.

Strength of numbers is the delight of the timid. The valiant in spirit glory in fighting alone.

I believe in God, not as a theory but as a fact more real than that of life itself.

Imperfect as I am, I started with
imperfect men and women
and sailed on
an uncharted ocean.

Indolence is a delightful
but distressing state; we must be
doing something to be happy. Action
is no less necessary than thought
to the instinctive tendencies
of the human frame.

The only tyrant I accept
in this world
is the still voice within.

Culture of the mind
must be subservient
to the heart.

If I had no sense of humor,
I would long ago
have committed suicide.

Perfect health can be attained only by living in obedience to the laws of God and defying the power of Satan. True happiness is impossible without true health, and true health is impossible without a rigid control of the palate. All the other senses will automatically come under control when the palate has been brought under control. And he who has conquered his senses has really conquered the whole world, and he becomes a part of God.

Strength does not come
from physical capacity. It comes from
an indomitable will.

The relation between the body and the
mind is so intimate that if either of
them got out of order, the whole
system would suffer. Hence it follows
that a pure character is the foundation
of health in the real sense of the term;
and we may say that all evil thoughts
and evil passions are but different
forms of disease.

INTER-
NATIONAL
PEACE

Mankind is one,
seeing that all are equally subject
to the moral law.
All men are equal in God's eyes.
There are, of course, differences
of race and status and the like,
but the higher the status of a man,
the greater is his
responsibility.

The golden way
is to be friends with the world and
to regard the whole human family
as one. He who distinguishes between
the votaries of one's own religion
and those of another
miseducates the members
of his own and
opens the way
for discord and irreligion.

There is no limit
to extending our services
to our neighbors
across State-made frontiers.
God never made those frontiers.

My goal is friendship
with the whole world, and I can
combine the greatest love
with the greatest opposition
to wrong.

If
there were no greed,
there would be no occasion
for armaments.
The principle of nonviolence
necessitates complete abstention
from exploitation
in any form.

As soon as the spirit
of exploitation is gone, armaments
will be felt as a positively unbearable
burden. Real disarmament cannot
come unless the nations of the world
cease to exploit one another.

I would not like
to live in this world
if it is not to be
one world.

The way of peace
is the way of truth. Indeed, lying is
the mother of violence. A truthful
man cannot long remain violent.
He will perceive
in the course of his search
that he has no need to be violent
and he will further discover
that so long as there is
the slightest trace of violence in him,
he will fail to find
the truth he is seeking.

The better mind
of the world desires today not
absolutely independent states warring
one against another, but a federation of
friendly, interdependent states.

In this age of brute force,
it is almost impossible
for anyone to believe
that anyone else
could possibly reject the law
of the final supremacy of brute force.

Peace cannot be built
on exclusivism,
absolutism,
and intolerance.

Interdependence
is and ought to be
as much the ideal of man
as self-sufficiency.

It is impossible
for one to be internationalist
without being a nationalist.
Internationalism is possible
only when nationalism
becomes a fact; for example,
when peoples belonging
to different countries
have organized themselves
and are able to act
as one man.

The West

is today pining for wisdom. It is despairing of a multiplication of the atom bombs, because atom bombs mean utter destruction, not merely of the West but of the whole world, as if the prophesy of the Bible is going to be fulfilled and there is to be a perfect deluge. It is up to you to tell the world of its wickedness and sin—that is the heritage your teachers and my teachers have taught Asia.

If the mad race for armaments continues, it is bound to result in a slaughter such as has never occurred in history. If there is a victor left, the very victory will be a living death for the nation that emerges victorious.

If we are to be saved and are to make a substantial contribution to the world's progress, ours must emphatically and predominantly be the way of peace.

It may be long
before the law of love will be
recognized in international affairs.
The machineries of governments
stand between and hide the hearts
of one people from
those of another.

A peace-bringer
must have a character
beyond reproach and must be known
for his strict impartiality.

Cenerally
there are previous warnings
of coming storms.
Where these are known,
the peace brigade will not wait
till the conflagration breaks out,
but will try to handle
the situation in anticipation.

I have found
that life persists in the midst of
destruction and therefore there must
be a higher law than that of
destruction. Only under that law
would a well-ordered society be
intelligible and life worth living.

I did not move
a muscle when I first heard that the
atom bomb had wiped out Hiroshima.
On the contrary, I said to myself,
"Unless now the world adopts
nonviolence, it will spell certain
suicide for mankind."

USAA
USAA INVESTMENT MANAGEMENT COMPANY

You can invest a specific amount each month in any of your accounts, including IRAs. Choose either the 1st or 15th of the month or both dates. Here's all you do: fill in the date, fund name and account number, and amount (minimum $50). Select either the 1st and/or the 15th of the month you wish the amount invested, and indicate your preferred date to start this service. **Please include a blank voided check or deposit slip from the bank account from which your investment will be made to give us your bank's address and routing number. Each listed account owner's signature must appear on the authorization form for this service.**

INVESTRONIC INVES

This authorization form must be

I authorize USAA Investment Management Compa in the following fund accounts:

Fund Name _____

Fund Account No. _____

Amount $ _____

Debit my account on: ☐ 1st ☐ 15th ☐ 1st &

Effective Date _____

Minimum investment per debit is $50 for each fund account. You ma regular fund account or an IRA. (For IRAs, make sure your total amm

Signature _____

Social Security Number _____

Signature of Joint Tenant (if any) _____

Social Security Number _____

I want to realize brotherhood or identity not merely with the beings called human, but I want to realize identity with all life, even with such beings as crawl on earth.

So long as one wants to retain one's sword, one has not attained complete fearlessness.

Peace
will never come
until the great powers
courageously decide
to disarm themselves.

Morality
is contraband
in war.

Noncooperation
with evil
is a sacred duty.

I regard
the employment of the atom bomb
for the wholesale destruction
of men, women, and children
as the most diabolical use
of science.

If we are to reach real peace in this world and if we are to carry on a real war against war, we shall have to begin with children; and if they will grow up in their natural innocence, we won't have to struggle; we won't have to pass fruitless, idle resolutions, but we shall go from love to love and peace to peace, until at last all the corners of the world are covered with that peace and love for which consciously or unconsciously the whole world is hungering.

DEMOCRACY

Self-government
means continuous effort to be
independent of government control,
whether it is foreign government or
whether it is national.

We must be content
to die
if we cannot live
as free men and women.

In matters of conscience,
the law of majority
has no place.

It is my certain conviction that no
man loses his freedom except through
his own weakness.

It is not so much British guns that are
responsible for our subjection as our
voluntary cooperation.

There is no bravery greater
than a resolute refusal
to bend the knee to an earthly power,
no matter how great, and that
without bitterness of spirit
and in the fullness of faith
that the spirit alone lives,
nothing else does.

The outward freedom
that we shall attain will only be in
exact proportion to the inward
freedom to which we may have grown
at a given moment. And if this is the
correct view of freedom, our chief
energy must be concentrated upon
achieving reform from
within.

The true
democrat is he who with purely
nonviolent means defends his liberty
and, therefore, his country's
and ultimately that of the
whole of mankind.

Democracy disciplined and
enlightened is the finest thing in the
world. A democracy prejudiced,
ignorant, superstitious will land itself
in chaos and may be self-destroyed.

My notion of democracy
is that under it the weakest
should have the same opportunity
as the strongest.
That can never happen
except
through nonviolence.

The true source of rights
is duty. If we all discharge
our duties, rights will not be
far to seek.
If leaving duties unperformed
we run after rights,
they will escape us
like a will-o'-the-wisp.
The more we pursue them,
the farther will
they fly.

To me political power
is not an end but one of the means of
enabling people to better their
condition in every department of life.

I believe
that true democracy can only be an
outcome of nonviolence. The structure
of a world federation can be raised
only on a foundation of nonviolence,
and violence will have to be totally
given up in world affairs.

119

What we want,
I hope, is a government not based on
coercion, even of a minority, but on
its conversion. If it is a change from
white military rule to brown, we
hardly need make any fuss.
At any rate, the masses
then do not count.
They will be subject
to the same spoliation as now,
if not even worse.

I value individual freedom, but you must not forget that man is essentially a social being. He has risen to his present status by learning to adjust his individualism to the requirements of social progress. Unrestricted individualism is the law of the beast of the jungle. We have learnt to strike the mean between individual freedom and social restraint. Willing submission to social restraint for the sake of the well-being of the whole society enriches both the individual and the society of which one is a member.

The golden rule
of conduct, therefore, is mutual
toleration, seeing that we will never
all think alike and we shall see Truth
in fragments and from different angles
of vision. Conscience is not the same
thing for all. Whilst, therefore, it is a
good guide for individual conduct,
imposition of that conduct upon all
will be an insufferable interference
with everybody's freedom of
conscience.

Differences of opinion
should never mean hostility.
If they did, my wife and I should
be sworn enemies of one another.
I do not know two persons in
the world who had no differences
of opinion, and, as I am
a follower of the Gita, I have
always attempted to regard
those who differ from me
with the same affection as I have
for my nearest and dearest.

]do not believe
in the doctrine of the greatest good of
the greatest number. It means in its
nakedness that in order to achieve the
supposed good of 51 percent, the
interest of 49 percent may be, or
rather, should be, sacrificed. It is a
heartless doctrine and has done harm
to humanity. The only real, dignified
human doctrine is the greatest good of
all, and this can only be achieved by
uttermost self-sacrifice.

A leader is useless
when he acts against the prompting
of his own conscience,
surrounded as he must be by
people holding all kinds of views.
He will drift like an anchorless
ship if he has not the inner voice
to hold him firm
and guide him.

The State
represents violence
in a concentrated and organized form.
The individual has a soul,
but as the State
is a soulless machine,
it can never be weaned
from violence,
to which it owes
its very existence.

In this age of democracy
it is essential that desired results are
achieved by the collective effort of the
people. It will no doubt be good to
achieve an objective through the effort
of a supremely powerful individual,
but it can never make the community
conscious of its corporate strength.

I firmly believe
that freedom won
through bloodshed or fraud
is no freedom.

The cause of liberty
becomes a mockery
if the price to be paid
is the wholesale destruction
of those who are to enjoy
liberty.

Liberty and democracy
become unholy
when their hands are dyed red
with innocent blood.

The real "white man's burden" is not
insolently to dominate colored or
black people under the guise of
protection; it is to desist from the
hypocrisy which is eating into them.
It is time white men learned to treat
every human being as their equal.

129

Mankind is at the crossroads. It has to make its choice between the law of the jungle and the law of humanity.

There is no human institution without its dangers. The greater the institution, the greater the chances of abuses. Democracy is a great institution and, therefore, it is liable to be greatly abused. The remedy, therefore, is not avoidance of democracy but reduction of the possibility of abuse to a minimum.

Good government
is no substitute
for self-government.

No culture can live
if it attempts to be exclusive.

One has to speak out
and stand up
for one's convictions.
Inaction at a time of conflagration
is inexcusable.

God may be called by any other name so long as it connotes the living Law of Life—in other words, the Law and the Lawgiver rolled into one.

The spirit of democracy cannot be established in the midst of terrorism, whether governmental or popular.

A man ends by becoming what he thinks, and it will be the same for India if she remains firmly attached to truth by means of love.

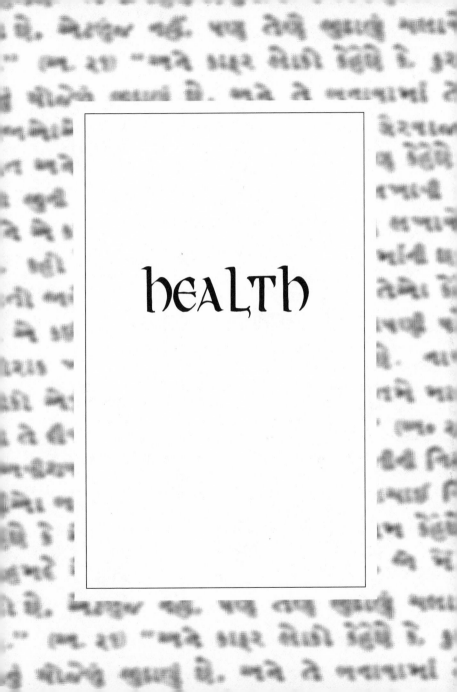

HEALTH

We want healers of souls rather than of bodies. The less we and others pamper our bodies, the better for us and the world.

The body which contains a diseased mind can never be anything but diseased.

Surely, those who spend their days in the worship of the belly are worse than the birds and the beasts.

I hope
that we will be concerned chiefly
with the prevention of diseases
rather than their cure.
The science of sanitation
is infinitely more ennobling.
I regard the present system as
black magic, because it tempts people
to put an undue importance
on the body
and practically ignores
the spirit within.

A clean spirit
must build
a clean body.

Indeed,
the body may be a good servant,
but when it becomes a master,
its powers of evil
are unlimited.

The world is compounded
of the five elements—
earth, water, air, fire, and ether.
So, too, is our body.
It is a sort of miniature world.
Hence the body stands in need of
all the elements in due proportion—
pure earth, pure water, pure fire or
sunlight, pure air, and open space.
When any one of these falls short
of its due proportion,
illness is caused in the body.

Thinking is the function of the mind,
and some people have called it
the eleventh sense.
In health, all the senses
and the mind
act in perfect coordination.

If we cultivate the habit
of keeping the air pure
and of breathing only fresh air,
we can save ourselves
from many a terrible disease.

Perfectly pure water
has a most beneficial effect
on the system; hence doctors
administer distilled water
to their patients.

Man can live
on wheat alone, for in it we have
in due proportion
all the elements of nutrition.

Man is not born to eat,
nor should he live to eat.
His true function is
to know and serve his Maker;
but, since the body is essential
to this service, we have perforce to eat.
Even atheists will admit
that we should eat
merely to preserve our health
and not more than is needed
for this purpose.

Skimmed milk is a very
valuable article of diet.

A certain amount of fat
is necessary. This can be had
in the form of ghee or oil.
If ghee can be had,
oil becomes unnecessary.

Tea, coffee, and cocoa
are all equally bad
in that they impair
the digestive powers.

Alcohol
makes a man forget himself,
and while its effects last,
he becomes utterly incapable
of doing anything useful.

Opium
is a well-known poison,
and its use as an intoxicant
should be strictly
prohibited.

I have no hesitation in saying
that the man who does not
eschew tobacco in all its forms
can never be perfectly healthy.

I do not regard flesh-food
as necessary for us at any stage
and under any clime in which it
is possible for human beings ordinarily
to live. I hold flesh-food to be
unsuited to our species.

If one may take
ripe fruit without cooking, I see no
reason why one may not take
vegetables, too, in an uncooked state,
provided one can properly
digest them.

The best time
for taking fruit
is in the early morning.

Indeed,
merely from the point of view of
health, it will be highly beneficial to
fast at least once a fortnight.

There is no necessity
to have more than three meals.
In the cities, some people keep on
nibbling from time to time.
This habit is harmful.
The digestive apparatus requires rest.

It is my firm conviction
that man need take no milk at all
beyond the mother's milk
that he takes as a baby.
His diet should consist of nothing
but sun-baked fruits and nuts.
He can secure enough nourishment
both for the tissues and the nerves
from fruits like grapes
and nuts like almonds. Restraint
of the sexual and other passions
becomes easy for a man
who lives on such food.

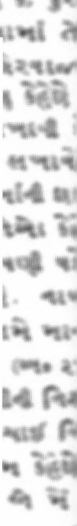

You will eat
not to satisfy your palate
but your hunger.
A self-indulgent man
lives to eat;
a self-restrained man
eats to live.

What do we mean
by *brahmacharya?* We mean by it that
men and women should refrain
from enjoying each other.
That is to say, they should not
touch each other with carnal thought;
they should not think of it
even in their dreams.
Their mutual glances should be free
from all suggestion
of carnality.

The law of Nature
is that *brahmacharya* may be broken
only when the husband and wife
feel a strong desire for a child.
Those who, remembering this law,
violate *brahmacharya*
once in four or five years
cannot be said to be slaves to lust,
nor can they appreciably lose
their stock of vitality.

The vast majority,
who may be numbered in thousands,
turn to sexual enjoyment
merely to satisfy their carnal passion,
with the result that children are
born to them quite against their will.
In the madness of sexual passion,
we give no thought
to the consequences of our acts.

So inextricably, indeed,
has venereal disease caught mankind
in its clutches
that even the best doctors have been
forced to admit that, so long as
adultery and prostitution continue,
there is no hope for the human race.
The medicines for these diseases are so
poisonous that although they may
appear to have done some good for the
time being, they give rise to other and
still more terrible diseases which are
handed down from generation to
generation.

Nocturnal dreams
need not cause any anxiety.
A cold bath every time
for a fairly strong person
is the finest preventive in such cases.
It is wrong to say
that an occasional indulgence
is a safeguard
against involuntary dreams.

The ideal kind of exercise is that which
gives vigor to the body as well as to the
mind; only such exercise can keep
a man truly healthy.

Our passion for exercise should become
so strong that we could not bring
ourselves to dispense with it
on any account.

The ability to sleep during odd
moments seems to be a necessity
in old age.

I think
it is the height of ignorance to
believe that the sexual act is
an independent function,
necessary like sleeping or eating.
The world depends for its existence
on the act of generation,
and as the world is the playground
of God and a reflection of His glory,
the act of generation should be
controlled for the ordered growth
of the world.

154

He who realizes this will control
his lust at any cost,
will equip himself with the knowledge
necessary for the physical, mental,
and spiritual well-being
of his progeny,
and give the benefit
of that knowledge
to posterity.

Though death and life are the faces
of the same coin, and though we
should die as cheerfully as we live,
it is necessary while there is life
to give the body its due.
It is a charge given to us by God.
And we have to take
all reasonable care about it.

A man who lives a life
of simplicity and chastity
will probably live long.

GLOSSARY

Ahimsa
Abstention from doing injury; nonviolence.

Brahmacharya
Observance of chastity in quest of God.
Vow of celibacy taken by Gandhi in 1906.

Satyagraha
Force born of truth or nonviolence.

Sutra
A short saying stating a general truth.

BIBLIOGRAPHY

Andrews, Charles Freer. *Mahtma Gandhi—
His Own Story.* New York: Macmillan, 1930.

Bok, Sissela. *A Strategy for Peace.* New York:
Pantheon Books, 1989.

Brown, Judith. *Gandhi: A Prisoner of Hope.*
New Haven: Yale University Press, 1989.

Chandra, Bipan. *India's Struggle for Independence,
1857–1947.* Delhi: Viking, 1988.

Dalton, Dennis. *Mahatma Gandhi: Nonviolent
Power in Action.* New York: Columbia
University Press, 1993.

Erikson, Erik. *Gandhi's Truth.* New York:
Norton, 1968.

Shirer, William. *Gandhi: A Memoir.* New York:
Simon and Schuster, 1979.

Philosophy Books From Carol Publishing Group

The Age of Reason by Thomas Paine, paperback $8.95 (#50549)

Albert Einstein: Letters to Solovine, paperback $8.95 (#51422)

The Bertrand Russell Dictionary of Mind, Matter & Morals, paperback $9.95 (#51400)

The Book of Gandhi Wisdom, compiled by Trudy S. Settel, paperback $6.95 (#51622)

The Christ: A fundamental study of Christianity's early development by Charles Guignebert, paperback $9.95 (#51143)

The Creative Mind: An Introduction to Metaphysics by Henri Bergson, paperback $8.95 (#50421)

The Dark Side: Thoughts on the Futility of Life From Ancient Greeks to the Present by Alan R. Pratt, paperback $10.95 (#51481)

Deceptions and Myths of the Bible by Lloyd M. Graham, paperback $14.95 (#51124)

The Diary of Soren Kierkegaard, paperback $7.95 (#50251)

Einstein on Humanism, paperback $8.95 (#51436)

The Emotions: Outline of a Theory by Jean-Paul Sartre, paperback $5.95 (#50904)

Essays in Existentialism by Jean-Paul Sartre, paperback $12.95 (#50162)

The Ethics of Ambiguity by Simone de Beauvoir, paperback $8.95 (#50160)

The Ethics of Spinoza: The Road to Inner Freedom, by Baruch Spinoza, paperback $10.95 (#50536)

Existentialism and Human Emotions by Jean-Paul Sartre, paperback $7.95 (#50902)

The Great Secret: What is the meaning of life? by Maurice Maeterlinck, paperback $7.95 (#51155)

The Life and Major Writings of Thomas Paine, paperback $15.95 (#50414)

Literature & Existentialism by Jean-Paul Sartre, paperback $6.95 (#50105)

Martin Buber's Ten Rungs: Collected Hasidic Sayings, by Martin Buber, paperback $6.95 (#51593)

The Mystery-Religions and Christianity by Samuel Angus, paperback $9.95 (#51142)

Out of My Later Years by Albert Einstein, paperback $10.95 (#50357)

Philosophers of China: Classical and Contemporary by Clarence Burton Day, paperback $5.95 (#50622)

The Philosophy of Existentialism by Gabriel Marcel, paperback $8.95 (#50901)

The Psychology of Imagination by Jean-Paul Sartre, paperback $8.95 (#50305)

Rights of Man by Thomas Paine, paperback $9.95 (#50548)

The Sayings of Muhammad by Allama Sir-Abdullah Al-Mamum Al-Suhrawardy, paperback $6.95 (#51169)

The Unfinished Dialogue: Martin Buber and the Christian Way by John M. Oesterreicher, paperback $5.95 (#51050)

The Way of Man: According to the Teaching of Hasidism, by Martin Buber, paperback $5.95 (#50024)

The World As I See It by Albert Einstein, paperback $7.95 (#50711)